# SUNSET
# SEEKING

# Find Inspiration in the Beauty of the Sun's Cycle

## By Hannah Seo

Cover Art by Cookie Moon
Interior Illustrations by Liana Jegers

# SUNSET
# SEEKING

CHRONICLE BOOKS

SAN FRANCISCO

POCKET NATURE SERIES

Text copyright © 2023 by **HANNAH SEO**.

Library of Congress Cataloging-in-Publication Data available.

ISBN 978-1-7972-1855-7

Manufactured in China.

MIX
Paper | Supporting responsible forestry
FSC™ C136333

Series concept and editing by **CLAIRE GILHULY**.
Series design by **LIZZIE VAUGHAN**.
Cover art by **COOKIE MOON**.
Interior illustrations by **LIANA JEGERS**.

Typeset in Albra, Benton Sans, Caslon.

Instagram is a registered trademark of Instagram LLC.

10 9 8 7 6 5 4 3 2 1

Chronicle books and gifts are available at special quantity discounts to corporations, professional associations, literacy programs, and other organizations. For details and discount information, please contact our premiums department at corporatesales@chroniclebooks.com or at 1-800-759-0190.

Chronicle Books LLC
680 Second Street
San Francisco, California 94107
www.chroniclebooks.com

# CONTENTS

Lo, now, the JOURNEYING SUN,
Another day's march done,
Kindles his campfire
at the edge of night!
And in the twilight pale
Above his CRIMSON TRAIL,
The stars move out their
cordons still and BRIGHT.

—**Bliss Carman,** from "The Campfire of the Sun"

Most people will see countless sunsets, and perhaps a few sunrises, in their lifetime, but only passively. When was the last time you *really* watched the sun rise or set? When did you last meditate on how the warm-toned reds and oranges give way to deep blues and purples, or how the different clouds cling to the light? Have you ever?

It's easy to take sunrises or sunsets for granted. After all, they happen with steadfast regularity, bookending the day in about twelve-hour intervals. But do not let the regularity of the sun fool you; every appearance and disappearance of the star on our horizon is a unique show. Each sunrise and sunset is an opportunity to witness transformation—the ever-shifting light means the sky is a different sky at every moment. Look away for too long, and you'll miss your favorite shade of burnt orange, or that faint sliver of green.

Anyone in the habit of watching the sun knows there's no platonic ideal of a sunset. The seemingly simple and predictable phenomenon of the setting sun can present itself with shocking variations—a winter sunset in Oslo, Norway is not the same as a summer sunset in Sydney, Australia. And there are so many variables at play that influence how both of those skies appear to the human eye.

As the sun moves across the sky—or rather, as the Earth rotates, angling different sections toward and then away from the sun's beams—there is a lot of interesting physics at play that yield a spectacle of colors. Sunlight interacts with our planet's atmosphere and the pollution in the air to scatter photons. Where you are in the world and what season it is changes the angles of light you'll witness. So not only is every evening an opportunity to witness an entirely new sunset, but each sunset is an entirely different sunset for every person watching in slightly different circumstances.

You may already be a keen sky-watcher, familiar with the variations and patterns of the sun's daily and seasonal transformations. Or maybe you've never closely watched a sunset before and feel underwhelmed by the idea of it. Whoever you are, this book will conjure, or re-conjure, the wonder and significance of the setting sun. In the following chapters, we will explore the physics of light scattering, how the Earth's tilted rotation brings seasons of extreme light and dark, how the setting sun impacts all life on Earth, and how cultures throughout time have honored the sun and its cycle. All this reminds us that sunsets are many things, but never mundane, and paying attention to one can be an art in itself, a practice in mindfulness and meditation. To that end, each chapter includes mindful exercises that encourage you to pause and turn your focus to the sun. Let these exercises serve as invitations to quiet your mind and observe the everyday beauty that nature provides.

You may think the name *Sunset Seeking* is a bit of a misnomer—after all, who needs to really search to find the sun in the sky? But, in this case, seeking a sunset is less of a *Where's Waldo?* exercise and more of a practice in observation and appreciation. When you seek a sunset and watch it with intention, you find something dynamic, full of depth, and surprisingly unpredictable.

While this book focuses first and foremost on sunsets, we will also address how the sun appears to us in the sky in its endless iterations. This includes sunsets, sunrises, and perhaps the odd solstice. After all, a sunset is simply one segment of the sun's constant but remarkable cycle. As we examine how the setting sun impacts the patterns of flora and fauna, the life of the planet, and our history and culture, be mindful of how sunsets play a role in your own life. A sunset can be an incredibly captivating phenomenon when you keep your eyes open and your mind engaged.

# MINDFULNESS

Try to remember the last sunset you really looked at. What comes to mind? Try to recall its progression, how the colors evolved as the day slipped into evening. Do you remember the context of the setting sun? How the landscape and life around you influenced the sky's appearance? If you don't, that's okay. Before you continue reading, take the time to watch the sunset today. Notice how all the variables interplay.

**WHILE GAZING AT A SUNSET, CONSIDER:**

## Colors

When you think of a sunset or sunrise, the dazzling colors likely come straight to mind. But take time to really note the kinds of blues, the intensity of the yellows, the variations of the reds as they bleed into other hues. How smooth or sharp are those gradients? At what point does one color become another? Can you see any individual rays of sunlight, and if so, what color are they?

---

## The skyscape
What else occupies the skyscape? Perhaps birds or planes are transecting the lines of color in the sky. If there are clouds, how are they positioned? How high or low are they? Are they moving? How do they interact with the sunlight, and are they taking on any color?

---

## The landscape
How does the landscape, urban or rural or in between, add to the scene? Are there reflections off buildings and cars? Are those reflections changing how bright it is, or how quickly nightfall seems to come? Is there green from trees or grass, or blue from water, and if so, how is that interacting with the light?

### Weather

Is there rain, haze, or fog? Light travels through space to get to your eyes, but different weather conditions can alter that journey and create different light and color conditions. How does weather impact how quickly the sun seems to rise or set?

A large drop of sun
lingered ON THE HORIZON
and then dripped over
and was gone, and
the SKY WAS BRILLIANT
over the spot
where it had gone…

—John Steinbeck, from *The Grapes of Wrath*

# I.

## WHAT MAKES A SUNSET?

**W**hat is a sunset, really? When does it start and end? After all, we sometimes say the sun is rising even before it peeps up above the eastward horizon. It continues to ascend until its noontime peak, and then begins its westward fall.

We talk about sunsets as if they are discrete events that happen at specific moments. But in reality, sunsets are a constant, perpetually shifting gradient as the Earth turns on its axis and moves parts of itself away from sunlight (or, in the case of sunrises, toward the sunlight). The light traverses in a never-ending cycle. An adventurous soul (who would need an impressive amount of stamina) could theoretically circle the globe chasing an endless sunset. Sunsets are therefore a process—different strips of the Earth are always passing the sunset baton over to their neighbors in an endless relay race.

But let's presume that each sunset is a unique and separate event. How do we define it? Where do we draw the lines? Well, the question of how to pinpoint a sunset is a surprisingly technical one. Forecasts generally say that sunset starts when the bottommost tip of the sun touches the horizon—and sunrises are the reverse, when the topmost tip of the sun touches the horizon. But there's a little more nuance to it.

Let's pretend we're on the equator, for the sake of simpler math. There, days are theoretically split evenly regardless of the season: twelve hours of day and twelve hours of night. When the sun is setting and the bottom of the sun touches down on the horizon, there's still plenty of light beaming out. From the moment that orb touches, it takes just two to seven additional minutes for the rest of the sun's body to make it below that line. And even once the entire sun is technically below the horizon, it'll still stay a little light out thanks to the way Earth's atmosphere bends the sun's rays—a phenomenon called *refraction*. Overall, the darkening of the sky can take up to an hour. A similar, reverse process happens for sunrise—the sky alights before the sun itself peeks above the horizon. The result: Daytime arrives two to seven minutes before the sunrise, and nighttime falls two to seven minutes after the sunset, making day up to fourteen minutes longer than night.

The day-night imbalance gets even more complicated once you move away from the equator. Based on your latitude, the angle between the Earth and sun changes, creating different theoretical expected day and night lengths. (The time of year also affects this, which we'll explore in chapter 2.) Plus, those calculations are based on flat-ish terrain. Add mountains and valleys to the equation, and the sunrise and sunset times you experience may feel quite different from those forecasted times.

REFRACTION

APPARENT POSITION OF SUN

YOU

HORIZON

ACTUAL POSITION OF SUN

LAYERS OF ATMOSPHERE

## WHY DO SUNSETS LOOK THE WAY THEY DO?

If you imagine a sunset, the picture that likely comes to mind is an orangey-yellow-red orb falling elegantly toward the horizon and washing the sky with an array of brilliant yellows and reds, followed by light and dark blues with the occasional splash of green. The through line: color.

Color is such a substantial part of why we are drawn to the sun and its daily journey. Color makes sunsets memorable and emotional. So what gives sunsets their distinctive kaleidoscope of hues? The answer is a physics phenomenon called Rayleigh light scattering, named after the British physicist Lord Rayleigh, who extensively studied the effect.

Sunlight contains all the colors on the spectrum, but when it shines in a vacuum, the wavelengths for different colors are locked and contained in those beams of light. We need something—like the particles of the atmosphere—to break the beams of light into rays of color. And even when we do see colors, we

# LORD RAYLEIGH SCATTERING

A ray of sunlight beaming in a vacuum, undisturbed, is not something you can actually see. That beam contains all the colors of the rainbow—the entire spectrum of visible light. In a vacuum, when the light isn't hitting anything, you only see the light waves that directly hit your eyes, bright and colorless. But once light enters the atmosphere, it pinballs off all the clutter in our air, like dust or gas molecules. All that reflecting unlocks colors from the beam, and those wavelengths reflect back at us, making color visible to human eyes.

In 1869, while studying infrared light, Irish physicist John Tyndall (who was the first to prove what would later be called *the greenhouse effect*) observed that when bright light hit different particulates in the air, the light became faintly blue-tinted. He hypothesized that this phenomenon may be related to why the sky is blue, but didn't pursue the issue further.

Lord Rayleigh, also known as John William Strutt, was a British physicist around the same time. Rayleigh was fascinated with waves of all kinds: sound waves, waves in fluids, light waves. In 1871, Rayleigh published two academic papers building off of what Tyndall had laid the groundwork for. In those papers, Rayleigh outlined how the sky polarizes light, or restricts the direction of light's vibrations, and how that yields differences of color. Over the next thirty years, as other scientists made further discoveries about how light works, Rayleigh refined his work.

He came up with a formula for light scattering that determines the colors a viewer will see depending on the kinds of molecules the light is bouncing off of. Using his equations, Rayleigh found that nitrogen and oxygen, the most abundant gases in the atmosphere, cause shorter wavelengths of light (like purples, blues, and greens) to be scattered much more widely than longer wavelengths of light (like reds and oranges), giving the sky its signature color. Meanwhile, when you glance directly at the sun, those less-scattered colors are more visible, so direct beams from the sun appear more yellow-red.

don't see them all in equal amounts. During sunrise and sunset, the angle of the sun's placement means that light needs to travel farther distances, through more of our planet's atmosphere, to get to viewers' eyes. Different layers of the atmosphere have different densities, so during sunrise and sunset, as light negotiates these changing densities, it bends and refracts more than it does at other times of the day. As the light makes its way through the gases and compounds in the atmosphere, it undergoes "scattering." All the individual photons, or light particles, bounce off of other particles in the air, like oxygen and nitrogen. Different photons with different wavelengths represent different colors, and the wavelength of each photon influences how it scatters. Photons with shorter wavelengths scatter more easily than those with longer wavelengths. Some photons get absorbed in clouds, some reflect back up into the atmosphere, and others make their way to Earth. It's not entirely unlike the way a rainbow forms: A whole beam of light gets split like an unraveling rope, its composite colors unbundle, and each color is unleashed as a separate entity. And as the light beams down and scatters in a multitude of directions, certain colors make their way through the fray better than others.

Blues and purples—colors with shorter wavelengths—are particularly prone to scattering. During sunrise and sunset, when photons have a longer journey through more atmosphere, there is so much scattering that these colors largely evade our eyes—they bounce all over the place, and much of that light gets reflected upward or absorbed into the sky. Meanwhile, reds, oranges, and yellows, which have longer wavelengths, go through much less scattering—just enough to make them visibly bounce around the sky, but not enough for the sky to absorb the light completely. It's this balance that gives us the pleasure of that brilliant, fiery show at dawn and dusk.

Clouds also end up reflecting the light and color that hits them. So as the sun sets and light is increasingly scattering, the clouds take on the growing multitude of colors. As the sun rises, the clouds will appear colorful before slowly bleaching as the sun travels higher and the light scattering lessens.

During a sunset, as the sun dips closer and closer to the horizon, it also gets farther and farther from the viewer, intensifying the scattering while also limiting the strength of the light. So the colors get more vivid even as the sky around it darkens. That said, there are many more factors that contribute to the varied brilliance of the sky at dawn and dusk, which we'll get to later on.

# MINDFULNESS

So, you've decided to watch the sun set. Hopefully, to give yourself ample time, you've settled into your observation spot a good half hour before the sunset is officially forecasted. It sounds like a lot of time, but half an hour of color-watching is half an hour well spent.

Relax your body, feel the muscles in your shoulders and back ease their grip, unfurrow your brow, and unclench your jaw. As you gaze at the sky, clear your mind, filling it only with the sights in front of you. As the sun arcs and dips, note the colors. Which ones do you see?

## Red

Red is oftentimes associated with aggression and passion, but stereotypes aside, think of how red really makes you feel. What objects, memories, or feelings come to mind? Perhaps you recall a tumultuous past life event, or maybe it elicits a sense of power. Does the sight of red in the sky alarm or excite you? Why or why not? Let it all bubble up, and sit with those feelings.

## Orange

Meditate on orange, a color that is frequently overshadowed by its primary color siblings. Sometimes heralded as the color of creativity and freedom, observe how streaks of orange change the sky's vibrancy. Orange is also the opposite color to blue on the color wheel. How does it feel to see so much orange above, in such stark contrast to the "normal" sky?

## Yellow

An alarming and uneasy color to some, but a joyful and optimistic color to others, yellow can be an ambiguous shade. Note how yellow acts as a bridge between the blues and greens and the oranges and reds. Observe where in the sky the yellow yields itself to one side or the other. Where does it hold its ground, taking up its own real estate?

## Green

Arguably the most overlooked color in the sky, green is special and sneaky. We rarely think of green as a color of the sunset, but of course it is. If the sky displays blues and yellows, there must also be greens. Look for the hidden greens, barely blended into the light above. At what point in the sunset do they show up the brightest? Can you catch the green before it disappears?

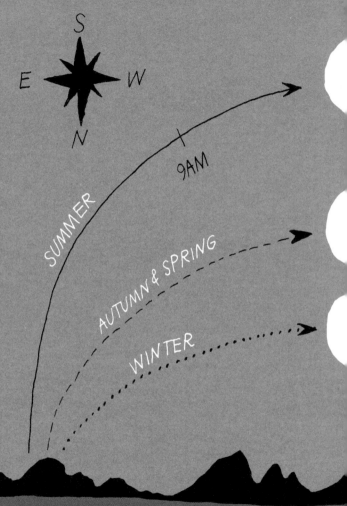

PATH OF THE SUN
THROUGH THE
SKY

NOON

3PM

SUNSET

Softly the evening came.
The sun FROM THE WESTERN HORIZON
Like a magician extended
his GOLDEN WAND o'er the
landscape;
TWINKLING vapors arose;
and sky and water and forest
Seemed all ON FIRE AT THE TOUCH,
and melted and mingled
together.

—**Henry Wadsworth Longfellow,** from "Evangeline"

# II.

## NO TWO SUNSETS ARE THE SAME

A regular sunset gazer knows that no two sunsets are ever exactly the same—even two sunsets observed in one place on consecutive evenings will look distinct. Each nightly dance of light is influenced by several factors. As we go through four of these variables—season, latitude, altitude, and pollution—think on how they might influence the sunsets where you live. And perhaps tonight, as you watch the sunset, you can observe these elements in action.

## SEASON

The time of year is one of the biggest and most well-known variables that impact sunsets. We all know that days are longer in the summer and shorter in the winter, meaning that sunsets happen later in the summertime and earlier in the winter months. But seasons also influence the duration of a sunset. The longest sunsets (and sunrises) happen at or near solstices, the days when the sun reaches its highest or lowest peaks in the sky. The solstices happen every year in mid-June and mid-December, and are the days with either the most or least amount of sunlight—in other words, they're the days when the Earth is tilted either closest or farthest away from the sun. That angle is the most extreme it will ever be, and as a result, the sunset gets dragged out, lasting more than a minute longer if you live around the middle of the United States (or anywhere in the world at that same latitude). Closer to the Arctic or Antarctic Circle, the solstice can extend the sunset for as many as twelve extra minutes.

Conversely, the shortest sunsets (and sunrises) occur at or near the equinoxes, in late March and September, when night and day are of almost equal length. On those days, the path of the sun across the sky happens at the steepest possible angle, and the center of the visible sun is directly above the equator, resulting in the shortest sunsets of the year.

Meteorologists also say that fall and winter sunsets are just . . . better. Ideal light scattering happens on a bell curve—not enough scattering and you don't get those reds and oranges, but too much scattering and all the colors become diffuse and muddy. The crispness of winter air, which is less humid, less polluted, and holds just a touch of moisture, makes for purer colors and is ideal for a sunset. During these seasons, the gradient of temperatures from north to south creates a cycle of air that's quite conducive to cloud formation. And remember, clouds reflect and take on the colors around them. The result is a stunning backdrop for a sunset.

Spring months tend to have less-brilliant sunsets, predominantly because of all the rain—the heavy water content of the air dulls the sky's hues, resulting in muted colors. Then, summer's heat and humidity are linked with pollution spikes that muddy the air. As the air cools down in the fall, the sunsets get better and better. But it's during winter, with the equinox well past, the solstice approaching or just barely gone, and the cold air blowing briskly, that all the ingredients are just right for an excellent sunset show.

## LATITUDE

So much of how the sun appears to us has to do with geometry and physics. Angles, reflections, refractions—all these things make up the delicate calculus of a sunset. So it shouldn't be surprising that latitude, or how far you are from the equator, is one of the most influential variables in how the sun performs in the sky. Latitude places you somewhere on the north-south axis of the Earth, and where you are in relation to the equator dictates the angles of the sun that you will be exposed to. In other words, where you sit latitudinally on the globe will change the kind of light show you can expect to see.

The sun sets and rises much more quickly near the equator than in northern or southern latitudes. Combine that with seasonal changes, and the duration of a sunset can vary dramatically. Near the Arctic Circle (65 degrees north in latitude), the duration of a sunset on the solstice can last about fifteen minutes. In the opposite conditions, at the equator (0 degrees latitude) on the equinox, the sunset will last a paltry one to two minutes.

But go far enough toward the poles and you may erase sunset (or sunrise) entirely. During Arctic summer (Antarctic winter), the North Pole is constantly bathed in light while the South Pole is blanketed in almost perpetual darkness. The sun does not fully disappear beneath the horizon up north, a phenomenon called midnight sun—it dips low, producing

PRACTICE

# MINDFULNESS

It's perfectly fine to take a photo of a sun-set—it's lovely to memorialize something beautiful with a photograph that will last and last. But when you find yourself on vacation in a beautiful new place, why not take that opportunity to really observe how this new sky differs from the one you see at home?

Before you snap a pic, go through the variables that make a sunset unique. What about your current environment makes the sunset different from the one you normally see? Are the colors of the sunset while you're vacation more beautiful and vivid, and if so, why? Is the sun setting faster or slower than you would expect?

Juxtapose this holiday sunset in your mind with the familiar sunsets of your home. What does the sunset in front of your eyes tell you about the place you are in? Perhaps the sky is more orange than you expected, signaling that maybe the area is experiencing a surge of pollution. Perhaps the colors are clear and clean, indicating a higher altitude.

This exercise is one way to really take in everything about this new place you are in. It's a way to appreciate an aspect of the natural world you may not regularly have access to. Even if you only do this once on your trip, it's worth the time. After all, there are things to observe that you won't necessarily be able to keep or record in a photo.

something like sunset, but continues to linger visibly near the Earth, keeping the land bright and colorful throughout the night. Then, the sun rises back high into the sky.

Meanwhile, during Antarctic winter, the sun makes the briefest of appearances. Daylight can last a paltry few hours, with the sun slowly peeking up above the horizon, then hanging low for a bit before starting its slow, too-soon descent back down. During Arctic winter (Antarctic summer), the opposite is true, with the South Pole bathed in light and the North Pole barely lit.

## ALTITUDE

At most latitudes on Earth, the effect of changing altitude alone is pretty simple and consistent in theory: The higher you go, the earlier the sun rises and the later it sets. This is again due to angles—the higher up you are, the more degrees of the Earth are in your field of vision. You can see farther. But most cities are not high enough for this to make any real difference, so unless you are atop a mountain or on a plane, these differences probably won't even register.

But one element of altitude that does have a big impact is the fact that the air is less dense the higher up you go. As the sun sets, the light will scatter and color will disperse as normal, but in the absence of pollution or particulates to absorb the scattered light, the colors will get to your eyes unobstructed, resulting in a brilliant show at the peak of its vibrancy. Places with lower altitudes often experience the opposite; the air is denser, and so the light tends to appear more dull and muted.

Mountains during colder seasons also have the added benefit of often being topped with snow and ice. All those reflective surfaces result in truly spectacular light shows. Mountaineers can also experience "alpenglow," the pink-red glow on the tops of mountains that appears at the end of and right after a sunset. As the sun submerges below the horizon, light beams hit clouds and ice particles in the

air, then indirectly hit the mountains. The result is a pinkish band of scattered, diffuse light emanating a soft glow. As the sun drifts further below the horizon, the mountains' halo turns purple, before everything finally rests in darkness.

## POLLUTION AND CLIMATE CHANGE

We know that the contents of the air change how light scatters and reflects. Pollution plays a big role in defining the contents and clarity of the air as the sun sets. Regular light scattering with just the natural particles and molecules in the air will yield some vivid colors, but the sky will never get too orange or too red. So where do those alarming, almost opaque warm tones come from? They're a product of pollution.

In the wake of the terrible wildfires in the western United States during the summers of 2020 and 2021, social media was awash with photos of *Mad Max*-esque hazy orange-red

# THE MOST INSTAGRAMMED SUNSETS IN THE WORLD

At the time of this writing, there are more than 260 million posts on Instagram using the #sunset hashtag—and there are surely many millions more photos without that tag. With their dazzling colors and shadows at play, it's no wonder that people are constantly trying to capture the glory of a sunset in a photo. Because sometimes it feels like if you photograph a moment, you can keep it forever. One website analyzed the staggering collection of sunset pics on Instagram to find which places were the most "grammed." Here are the results.

---

1. **CALIFORNIA, UNITED STATES**
   With a whopping 5.7 million sunset pics on record, the Golden State tops out the list. Considering that the state is full of valleys, greenery, long

coastlines, and social media savants, it's not too surprising that Californians proudly and frequently document their skies.

---

2. **SICILY, ITALY**
The Italian island of Sicily, situated on the Mediterranean, is the runner-up in this list. This popular vacation destination is known for its temples, beaches, delicious pizza . . . and apparently sunsets. The island is home to Mount Etna, and gazing at the sun as it lowers behind the iconic mountain is a popular tourist activity.

---

3. **BALI, INDONESIA**
Taking the bronze is the lush landscape of Bali, Indonesia—a particularly popular destination for beach getaways. According to travel bloggers, Bali sunsets are singular explosions of color, with just enough cloud cover and light scattering to truly experience a whole rainbow of sky.

---

4. **PARIS, FRANCE**

---

5. **SYDNEY, AUSTRALIA**

---

6. **LONDON, ENGLAND**

---

7. **MOSCOW, RUSSIA**

---

8. **MUMBAI, INDIA**

---

9. **PHUKET, THAILAND**

---

10. **IBIZA, SPAIN**

IBIZA, SPAIN —

CALIFORNIA, UNITED STATES

POPULAR PLACES TO CATCH A SUNSET

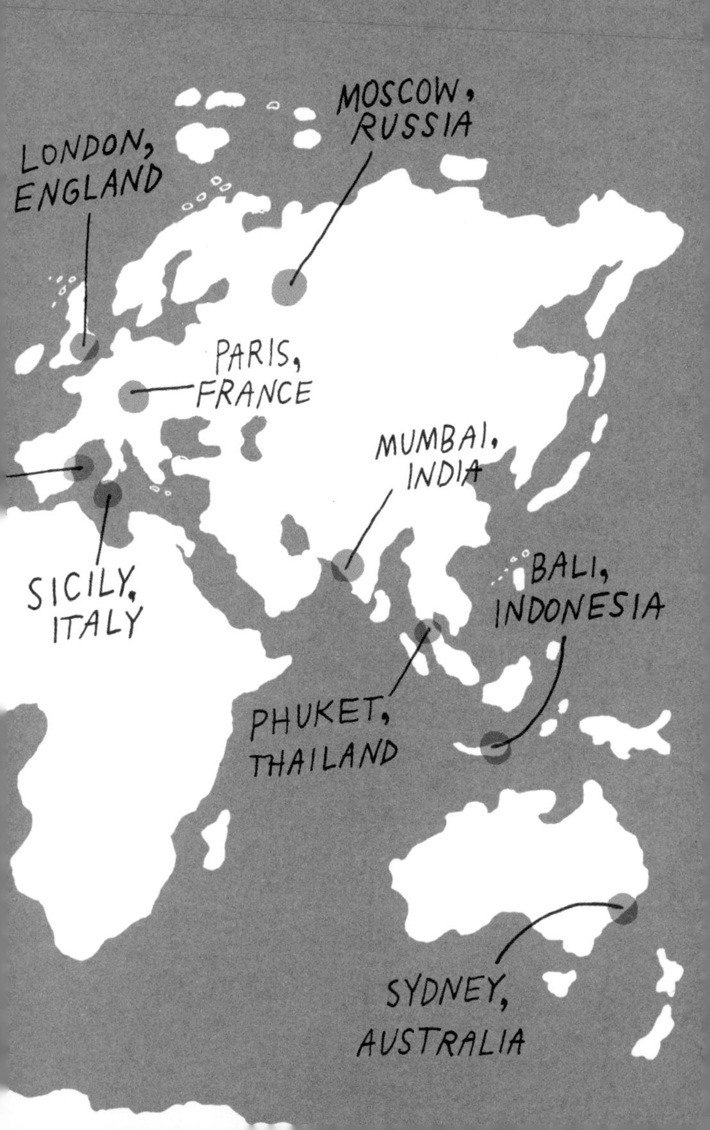
MOSCOW,
RUSSIA
LONDON,
ENGLAND
PARIS,
FRANCE
MUMBAI,
INDIA
SICILY,
ITALY
BALI,
INDONESIA
PHUKET,
THAILAND
SYDNEY,
AUSTRALIA

skies. The blaze of fires filled the air with soot and smoke. Those particulates shot all the way up the atmospheric column, reaching 50,000 feet [152,400 m] into the stratosphere. Only thick pollution containing aerosols and particulates can ramp light scattering up to the max; all the color from sunlight ricochets out, leaving only the longest wavelengths of light—the oranges and reds.

It might be easy to then jump to the conclusion that air pollution enhances the beauty of a sunset. That's not necessarily true, though that urban legend has existed for years now. Polluted skies do result in more reds and oranges, but those colors tend to be muddier than the ones seen in places with cleaner atmospheres. Ambient pollutants can yield vivid colors, but those colors also tend to come with haze and low visibility, making sunsets murkier and less dazzling.

Polluted skies at sunset are colorful but washed out and hazy to the point where you lose a lot of clarity and definition. For example, in California post-fire, you can sometimes not even see the sun. Excessive red and orange sunsets are an indication of lesser air quality, even if the colors seem exciting and fun. Some may find this sight more beautiful, but meteorologists and other skyscape connoisseurs (and now you) know that clean skies and pure colors should be valued more.

Fossil fuels and greenhouse gas pollution are changing the climate, and every aspect of the Earth is being affected, including sunsets. As air quality worsens, water clarity dulls, and greenery gives way to concrete, perhaps we can expect our sunset skies to gradually grow redder, less vibrant, and less reflective.

# SCIENTISTS USED PAINTINGS TO STUDY VOLCANO SKIES

In 2014, scientists analyzed hundreds of sunset paintings done between 1500 and 2000 CE. During that five-hundred-year period, fifty large volcanic eruptions happened around the world, and master painters documented those glowing skies.

The research team looked at the ratios of reds and greens in the paintings, which revealed interesting environmental information. Those red-green ratios correlated with the amount of volcanic aerosols in the atmosphere, regardless of the painter and style of artwork—when historical air quality records indicated skies with more volcanic ash, artists tended to paint with more reds than greens.

Scientists then asked a modern master painter and colorist to take a stab at painting two sunsets on the island of Hydra on the Aegean Sea.

Unbeknownst to the artist, one of the selected painting days was a normal day, while the other was just after a dust storm. The artist presented works with red-green ratios that matched those found in those older artworks.

Knowing this pattern exists in artworks is not just a quirky way to see how painters interpret the skies they see. The researchers say this could be a great tool to further our understanding of how the skies have changed throughout history. By examining artworks depicting sunsets through-out history, it could be a way to extrapolate the quality of the air in different places over time when we don't have written records. Plus, having historical atmospheric data—even from just these painting color ratios—provides opportunities to understand a fuller story of our Earth's air quality, which in turn will allow scientists to create better models when predicting the future of our climate.

The **SUN**
has gone
**TO BED** and
so must I.

—from "So Long, Farewell," *The Sound of Music*

# III.

## THE SUN & I

The sun, our planet's one source of light, has incredible influence over our biology and the biology of all of Earth's flora and fauna. Evolutionary scientists often cite light and heat as two of the most critical factors that allowed life on our planet to flourish. Beyond giving life, the sun and its cycle also dictate a number of variables for how we humans go about our day-to-day lives.

## OUR SUN THE TIMEKEEPER

One of the most fundamental roles of the sun in our society is as a timekeeping signal. Time is a human construct, and tracking the sun and its shadow is a universal way people have defined the progression of the day and its transformation into night.

The invention of the sundial led people to break down the day into hours. The first, rudimentary sundials were mere sticks staked into the ground, invented as early as 3500 BCE by some estimates. By 1500 BCE, the Ancient Egyptians had moved on to create the earliest portable sundials, which were designed with marks around the circumference to divvy the day up into segments. The *T*-shaped Egyptian sundial divided the day in half: when the sun was rising versus when the sun was setting. Each half was divided further into six parts, making the day twelve hours long. They then split night into another twelve sections. The Egyptians were fond of the duodecimal system—a notation system that uses twelve as its base. Their splitting of day and night into twelve equal parts each is how we arrived at twenty-four hours in a day.

The Ancient Egyptians had the benefit of living in a place with fairly consistent sunlight. The sun's path in the sky gets more consistent throughout the year the closer you get to the equator. For other cultures and societies up north or down south, closer to the polar regions, telling time with the sun is a little trickier. During polar summers, the sun sometimes doesn't set at all, making it light out for all twenty-four hours. During polar winters, you might see just a couple hours of daylight.

Populations in Scandinavia would tell time with "daymarks." They would split the horizon up into eight cardinal directions and sub-directions and use landmarks in each of those sections to note how the sun was traveling through the sky. When the sun rose, the nearest mountain or waterfall or other land feature was used to mark the "rise-measure place." When the sun set, on the other side of

# MINDFULNESS

If you live somewhere with a good enough view, try determining your own daymarks. What buildings or points of interest lie around where the sun sets? Notice whether the sun descends in a different location depending on the changing seasons—how does that compare to the anchor of your daymark? Then, as you observe and map out the path of the sun, see how your energy and activity throughout the day correlates. Where in relation to your daymarks do you feel the most rejuvenated, and where do you start to wane? Are there places in the day, following the arc of the sun, where your energy diverges from the sun's path? And if so, what does that say about your body's natural rhythms?

the horizon, the nearest landmark was used to mark "mid-evening's place." During summer, even though the sun is high in the sky and hardly (if ever) sets, it would still reach the rise-measure place and mid-evening place at the same times. So even without a sunset, in the summer, they could still tell what time of the evening it was. Time telling was harder in the winter, though, as the sun stayed below the horizon for most of the day.

## SUNSET AND FLORA/FAUNA

Sunrise and sunset are pretty big phenomena—the arrival and departure of light is a big event for living creatures, animals, and plants alike. A vast majority of life on Earth relies on this cycle, and most living beings have internal circadian rhythms that follow to match the day or night.

As just one small example, young sunflowers usually face east to greet the sun when it

rises. The flowers turn to keep their faces in line with the sun as it moves across the sky during the day. By the time the sun sets, the flowers are facing west, and once it's dark, the young sunflowers spend the night slowly returning to their eastward position. Older sunflowers aren't as mobile, and eventually they freeze in their east-facing position. But in their earliest days, both sunrise and sunset are important signals in the plant's daily routine.

By studying organisms in places with differing sunset conditions, scientists can get a glimpse of the secret cycles of plants. When a team of Finnish and Austrian researchers turned their novel terrestrial laser scanning technology onto birch trees, they found some surprising results. Once sunset fell, tree branches relaxed, drooping as much as 4 inches [10 cm]. Just before dawn began, those branches would pick back up, resuming their daytime positions. While they're not certain whether it is sunlight that is exactly triggering these cycles, researchers feel like changes in light act as some sort of signal to cue the trees to wind down.

# MINDFULNESS

It's strange, perhaps even counter-intuitive, to think of a place at night as almost a different habitat than that same place during the day. But the wild activity of a place can look vastly different from day to night, a testament to how life is so reactive to the quality of sunlight around it. As night approaches, wherever you are, try to spot and appreciate those changes. Perhaps different bugs populate the air. Maybe certain birds return to their nests, giving more airspace to fruit bats. The sunset is an opportunity to acknowledge not only the shifts of color in the sky, but also the shifts in life all around us.

When sunset doesn't arrive as expected, it can throw some animals' lives off balance. When zoos and aquariums house creatures from different parts of the world, they need to replicate the sun and moon cycles from their native homes to keep them healthy. When a zoo in North Carolina received Arctic puffins, they noticed how their molting behaviors changed. Ordinarily, puffins shed their wing feathers in the wintertime as days shorten and sunsets arrive earlier and earlier. Most puffins were kept in an area with light timers to replicate the Arctic sun—they molted just fine. But a couple birds held in the back for veterinary care were exposed to local North Carolina daylight hours. Those puffins didn't molt that year when they were supposed to.

As the sun descends, the increasing darkness triggers movement in the sea as well as on land. Every night, all kinds of marine species rise up from the depths to shallower waters and then retreat back down as sunrise approaches—a phenomenon called diel vertical migration. Creatures ranging from zooplankton, krill, and

gelatinous salps all the way to bigger fish and sharks vertically migrate on a daily basis. Shallower waters contain marine plants to feed on as well as mating grounds, and scientists think creatures travel after sunset so they can avoid predators that rely on sight to attack. For all the hopeful migrators trekking in the safety of dark, sunset is the signal for the all-clear.

## SUNSETS AND MOOD

The sun literally changes our bodies' biology.

If we lived in a wholly natural world, devoid of artificial light, our bodies' biological clocks would synchronize to solar time. As the sun descends, energizing external blue light levels decrease, signaling to our bodies that day is giving way to night. Our bodies would slowly but noticeably wind down, preparing for slumber, settling into "biological night." That downtime would give our bodies just enough rest before we'd begin to wake up.

66

But in our world of electricity and light bulbs, our daytime sunlight exposure diminishes, and our nighttime light exposure shoots up. The result is a skewed biological clock that doesn't quite know when to drift into rest. Think of how jarring it can be when you're inside all day and suddenly realize that it's dark out. Mentally shifting to the evening that way can be challenging. Being outside to witness the sky's evolution from day to night helps your body gently ease into that transition.

Sunlight has been heralded throughout history as an amazing curative force for human health. Even Hippocrates, one of the fathers of medicine, acknowledged the sun's power. He routinely prescribed sunbaths for his patients. Stories say that Florence Nightingale, the founder of modern nursing, once protested the design of a hospital because it wouldn't allow for sunlight to penetrate the wards. These historical figures knew intuitively what centuries of science would later prove: that exposure to our sky's natural light cycles can speed up healing and restore balance in the body.

On the other hand, inadequate sun exposure and disturbed biological clocks can worsen mental health and exacerbate existing conditions. Seasonal affective disorder, for example, frequently hits people during fall and winter, brought on by the shrinking day.

Disrupted light schedules can worsen symptoms in patients with dementia and Alzheimer's disease. "Sundowning" is a state of confusion that happens late in the afternoon and into the evening or night. Many people with dementia have worsened symptoms during this time and can get especially anxious, aggressive, or restless. The thing that helps mitigate sundowning the most? Light exposure throughout the day, and a predictable wind-down routine as evening approaches. For sundowners, a prolonged decrease in light over time is much better than the stark change from light to dark we often get when we're only exposed to artificial light.

Mindfully observing a sunset can help bring even healthy people into the present and provide a sense of prolonged time. Recent

# MINDFULNESS

Oscar Wilde once said, "Everything in moderation, including moderation." Of course, the sun was here long before Wilde spoke these words, but it's interesting how it follows suit. The sun is, in many ways, measured and reliable, but the existence of polar night and midnight sun show how (predictably) extreme it can be at times. Think of the extremes in your daily life. Are they predictable? Do you follow cycles of extremes and moderations, and if so, do they work to serve the ultimate balance in your life? If not, how do you return to a place of balance?

research shows that when people experience a sense of awe at a natural phenomenon, they feel "time rich"—they are less impatient and say they feel like they have an abundance of time. People who frequently experience this kind of awe also tend to be more generous and more satisfied with life. In addition, they generally feel more at peace with themselves and their lives, are more inclined to help others, and experience general greater well-being. Letting the sunset awe you, therefore, is a practice in wellness.

## AREAS OF EXTREME SUN

We tend to think of sunsets as immutable facts. No matter what happens, the sun will set and the sun will rise, say greeting cards and mindfulness posts. These platitudes find their way to Instagram posts, home decor, and even media —"The sun will come out tomorrow," sings the orphan Annie.

But the reality is, in some places, the sun does not always set and does not always rise. As we discussed in chapter 2, if you traverse north toward the Arctic Circle or south toward Antarctica, you'll find regions where summer nights are illuminated by the midnight sun (a sun that never fully sets), and the winters are washed in polar night (when the sun never rises).

So many creatures rely on sunlight to regulate their biological clocks, including humans. This has made biologists especially keen to see how different creatures cope in areas of extreme sun. Do the lines between nocturnal and diurnal species blur at all? Does the strain of prolonged light or prolonged dark impact health or quality of sleep? While most people manage to adapt just fine to both midnight sun and polar night, some experience insomnia, restless sleep, and fatigue.

Areas of extremes make for exciting scientific exploration. Zooplankton, which make daily vertical migrations typically thought to be triggered by the changing light, continue to make their migrations in polar regions despite constant sun or constant darkness. What that tells marine biologists is that there is no one ruling trigger for these patterns. Bodies and light are always in conversation, and other factors are at play as well.

# MINDFULNESS

In our world of fast-changing content, watching the sky for even just ten minutes may not seem like a worthwhile endeavor. But in the scale of a full day, ten minutes is a small fraction, and spending even just ten minutes outside, away from screens and in the natural world, can improve your mental well-being.

As you watch the sun dip, think about all the factors that have brought the light and color of this specific sunset to your eyes. Think of where you are on the planet, and how the beams of the sun have traveled through the vacuum of space, then the atmosphere of the Earth, then the air of wherever you are, to arrive in your line of sight. That's 93 million miles [150 million km] of journeying, plus all the chaos of light bouncing and reflecting and scattering, to get to your eyes.

Cosmically, everything about a sunset is a statistical anomaly. Not every planet has a sun. Not every planet has an atmosphere. Each sunset is unique and will never be repeated. How lucky are we to experience such a wonder?

I'll tell you how the SUN ROSE,
A ribbon at a time.
The steeples SWAM IN AMETHYST,
The news like squirrels ran.
THE HILLS untied their bonnets,
The bobolinks begun.
Then I said SOFTLY TO MYSELF,
"That must have been
the sun!"

—**Emily Dickinson,** from "I'll Tell You How the Sun Rose"

# IV.

## THE MYTHS OF THE SETTING SUN

The sun moves with such regularity that it's easy to take it for granted and see it as something mundane. But the sunset and sunrise are fantastic events, and people throughout time and across geographies have wondered what fuels the sun's travels. Without the cosmic knowledge of planetary orbits, it's easy to be awed by how special this cycle is. And to think that we, Earth's inhabitants, are gifted this regular light and spectacular color show each morning and night!

Different cultures have used a diverse assortment of mythical explanations to make sense of natural phenomena, including the sun's cycle. Myths act as both belief system and entertainment—a way for a people to imbue the world around them with narrative and meaning. These myths can also reveal a culture's structure of values.

Many cultures saw the sun as the pinnacle of virtue and value. It is often associated with truth, royalty and nobility, honor, justice, war, and the creation of life. The character of the sun was often portrayed as a traveler, chaser, or seeker of some sort. And while in the Western world today the sun is often thought of as male and the moon female, many ancient cultures had female sun deities. Some cultures have just one sun god, while others have multiple—there are almost thirty different sun gods across multiple belief systems in the Philippines, representing different iterations of the sun in the sky.

Here is a sample of just a few sun gods from throughout the world over time, and a few myths that have been spun around the setting sun.

### GNOWEE

In the mythology of various Aboriginal tribes of southeastern Australia, Gnowee is a solar goddess.

According to the Wotjobaluk people, there was a distant time when the world was eternally dark. Back then, people could only move about when they carried torches made of flaming tree bark. Gnowee was a woman then. One day, she needed to go dig for yams, but her little son was sleeping. She didn't want to leave him, but food was scarce, so she waited until he was asleep and went out to search, torch in hand.

Gnowee's hunt for food proved difficult, and her search took her farther and farther from her sleeping son. She wandered so far that she reached the end of the Earth, passed under it, and emerged on the other side. Disoriented and confused, Gnowee didn't know where she was. She started scrambling for a path back but she couldn't seem to find her way. To get a better view, she climbed into the sky, but still couldn't find where she left her son. To this day, she wanders with her torch, lighting the whole world as she continues to try and reunite with her child.

When Gnowee has traversed the whole sky, she takes her search underground. The setting sun is Gnowee making her way back under the Earth, traveling all the way around before emerging again on the other side. While she is above ground, her torch lights our day and allows us to thrive, and while she is underground, her torch brings warmth and fertility to the planet, allowing plants and animals to flourish.

Other Aboriginal populations in Australia have similar Gnowee myths. The Milingimbi people, who traditionally lived in an area where

the sun appears to set into the ocean, have
a myth where Gnowee turns into a great
Warrukay fish once she reaches the ocean. She
then swims under the Earth to return in the
east the next morning. In other versions of the
myth, Gnowee's journey is simply a daily rit-
ual. Lighting her torch provides the first light
of dawn, and before setting off, she decorates
herself with powdered red and orange pigments, coloring the clouds with warm hues in
the process. In the evening, she finds she must
renew her pigments, spilling more reds and
yellows into the sky again for sunset before
she begins her long passage underground back
to her campsite.

In these myths, the meaning of sunsets
is twofold. Sunset represents the point where
Gnowee has to turn back, signaling futility,
but also persistent hope. It is also the opportunity for the Earth to revitalize itself—Gnowee,
the sun, and her sheer persistence and tireless-
ness fuels the Earth and gives it strength.

## HELIOS

In Greek mythology, Helios is the god and personification of the sun. His Roman counterpart is Sol.

The Greeks envisioned Helios as a god driving a chariot across the sky, pulled by four white horses. Some sources describe his chariot as gold or pink. He conducts his daily rides out of duty, while also observing all the happenings on Earth. The Horae, the goddesses of the seasons, serve as Helios's advisers, helping him yoke his chariot on a daily basis. Every morning, his sister Eos, the goddess of dawn, opens the gates of heaven for Helios to begin his journey.

Personifying the sun as a godly person helped the Greeks explain variations in day lengths and sunsets. Summer days were longer, the Greeks thought, because Helios liked to stop his chariot mid-flight to watch the nymphs dance in the sun. On winter mornings, it was thought that he lingered in bed with his consort, prolonging the darkness and shortening the day.

How Helios performs sunset itself is disputed among sources. Helios is sometimes referred to as a water-lover since, from the Greeks' perspective, he rose and fell into the ocean in his daily cycle. Some sources say that sunset happens as Helios rides his chariot into the water. When he splashes down, he makes his way into the underground, traveling back east in the darkness. Other sources say that, at the hour of sunset and upon reaching the ocean's surface, Helios climbs in a giant cup made of solid gold. Inside this golden cup he rests, sailing back east as the chalice bobs up and down on the Mediterranean. A third version of the story, told by bards of Ancient Greece, says that once Helios reaches the west, he lies not in a golden cup, but in a boat or a

bed forged by Hephaestus, the god of black-
smiths and craftsmen, which gently shuttles
the sleeping sun god back east through the
night.

In addition to Helios, the sunset was
personified by the Hesperides, the goddess-
nymphs of evening and the golden light of
sunsets. Also known as the daughters of Nyx,
the goddess of night, the Hesperides were said
to live in the westernmost lands where they
protected a garden of golden apples. As Helios
broaches the western lands, his light mingles
with the glow of the Hesperides and their
apples, creating sunset's signature warmth and
vibrancy.

Helios is in many ways a calmer embod-
iment of the sun than those in some other
cultures. The fact that most Greek myths
have him resting after sunset means his daily
schedule mirrors our own. Busying ourselves
during the day and resting once the sun is
down, we follow Helios's example.

UTU

Utu, later worshipped by the Babylonians as Shamash, was the ancient Mesopotamian sun god and the twin brother of Innana, Queen of Heaven. While Gnowee's daily sky travels are motivated by a constant search, and Helios's chariot rides are a daily duty, Utu was said to be a steward of justice.

Utu travels the sky every day in a chariot. His light, the ancient Mesopotamians said, made all things visible. As he looks on, Utu observes every action on Earth, taking tallies and meticulously noting every human affair. A benevolent god, Utu often helps those he spots in need; some myths say he helped couples conceive children, while others say he protected families in floods. As Utu descends for sunset, his role turns from a watcher and guardian to a dispenser of justice. He enters the underworld and hands out judgment there based on his observations of the day. Meanwhile, Utu travels slowly back east, preparing for the next day ahead.

This Mesopotamian belief system highlights a common theme in cultures around the world: Light and the sun are associated with truth and goodness. The Ancient Egyptians' sun god Ra similarly travels the underworld at night to help ferry souls and dispense judgment. In both myths, the transition from day to night accompanies multiple transformations: The sky itself changes, but so do the gods' roles. Day is for watching over the living; night is righting wrongs in the darkness of the underworld.

Before the discovery of the solar system, it makes sense that sunset would be depicted as a god's descension below the Earth—after all, that's what it looks like. But these myths also add purpose to the transition between day and night, giving their protagonist gods different heroic objectives during their underground cycle. Sunset becomes a necessary transformation, demarcating the functional difference between day and night.

BEAIVI

Beaivi is the sun deity of the Sami people, the Indigenous people of northern Scandinavia. While Beaivi is most often depicted as female, some accounts record Beaivi as male.

The Sami have traditionally lived in places that experience polar night and midnight sun, and so the sun deity is revered a little differently than in cultures where the sun has a more consistent presence. Like in other cultures, the sun is associated with the fertility and vitality of plants and animals. But unlike in other cultures, Beaivi also represents sanity, as the Sami believe that the sun has powers to protect the mind and cure madness.

During polar night, when darkness persists around the clock and the sun never broaches the horizon, it's common to experience strain on one's mental health. So on the winter solstice, the darkest day of the year, the Sami traditionally sacrifice a white animal (usually a reindeer) in honor of Beaivi and to ensure she will safely return to the world.

It makes sense that generations of people living in a part of the world where the sun doesn't shine for months on end would begin to pray to the sun to heal their mentally ill. During the autumn months, the days shorten, and those near the North Pole have to watch as the sun's arc in the sky gets shorter and weaker day by day. As polar night approaches, sunset to them must be accompanied with a different mixture of emotions. One day, the sun barely hops out above the horizon; another day, the sun just sits on the skyline like one prolonged sunset. And then, the farewell—Beaivi disappears altogether, weak and resting.

As springtime approaches and the sun returns, the Sami traditionally smear butter on their doorposts, an offering to Beaivi that allows her to gain strength as she climbs higher and higher in the sky. The days lengthen as Beaivi convalesces, and as she grows stronger, Beaivi in turn confers strength to others—the reindeer, and the plants, and the Sami people who have waited patiently for her return.

## TSOHANOAI

Tsohanoai is the sun deity from Navajo mythology. He is the most important male deity in the Navajo tradition, and basically the mythological equivalent of Zeus, Apollo, Cronus, and Saturn combined. Perhaps out of reverence for this mighty god, people don't impersonate Tsohanoai or depict him in art like they do with other gods.

Tsohanoai is sometimes described as a man, hunched over, lugging the large sun on his back as he walks across the sky. Other times, he is described as a warrior on horseback, the blue steed of the sky, riding and holding the sun as a gleaming shield. In both cases, sunset is the same conclusion to daily travel: Tsohanoai eventually reaches his house situated out in the western lands and hangs the sun up inside on the western wall. Tsohanoai spends the evening in his house with his wife.

It's unclear how Tsohanoai gets back to the east in time for sunrise, or why he has been charged with this daily pilgrimage. But this myth, like those of Utu and Helios, nicely mirrors people's daily lives. Sunset is a home-coming, a time to halt labor and wandering and instead turn to home and hearth.

Like Gnowee, Tsohanoai does not embody the sun, but rather carries it as he crosses the sky. In this context, sunset signals balance: a tool is laid to rest, and the work is temporarily done.

. . .

Surveying the mythologies of the sun across cultures reveals the commonalities in the interpretations that humans have held across space and time.

Sometimes the sun *is* a god, the personification of light and warmth, like in the case of Helios, Beaivi, and Utu. These deities tend to act watchers, stewards of the day. With their presence comes some sort of societal or biological benefit; the sun therefore represents health or order or justice. But in other myths, the sun is an object to be carried. Gnowee and Tsohanoai both bring the sun along with them in their travels—Gnowee as she scours in her perpetual quest, Tsohanoai in his daily laborious commute. The sun in these cases becomes a tool that guides our purpose, a thing that brings light and warmth and life. So the thing to be praised and admired is not the sun, but the bringer of the sun.

The theme of work and labor is also common in sun mythology. Helios, Utu, and Tsohanoai all travel the sky because it is their duty. And like most human days, labor is designated to daytime, while nighttime has alternate purpose—either rest or righting the wrongs of the day. In these cases, the mythology sends a clear message: Work is for the day alone.

Regardless of how or why the sun travels its daily route, sun mythology consistently signals the importance of the sun for our own health and well-being, but also frequently the Earth's. The sun's presence comes with vitality and warmth, obviously, but also order, peace, sanity, and hope. Its setting, in turn, comes with transformation, homecoming, and rest.

As you watch the sun in your own life and its path down to the horizon, think about the myths of the setting sun. Which bring you comfort, and why? Which, when you reflect on them, seem to mirror the transformations and arcs in your own life? Regardless of what your belief system is, watching the sunset is an opportunity to assess how you feel about the day that has just passed, and how you want to feel for the night and following day ahead.

The STAR OF DAY,
pale but nevertheless
still splendid,
was setting
in the HORIZON,
glorifying at once
the heavens
and the sea
with BANDS OF FIRE...

—**Alexandre Dumas,** from *The Three Musketeers*

# V.

## WHAT WE CAN LEARN
## FROM THE SUN'S CYCLE

The sun and its cycle are so much more complex and nuanced than many of us may initially believe. Sunsets are especially deceptive. What may seem a simple and repetitive event actually involves a multitude of factors and has inspired story after story. From meditations on cycles to conversations about timescales, this chapter offers a few lessons and takeaways that will hopefully further deepen your appreciation of the sun.

## MOTHER EARTH > MANKIND

Ask anyone how they feel about sunsets and the answer will most likely be vaguely positive, or perhaps a little ambivalent. It's kind of fair—although the sunset is pretty much the only time you can see such a huge display of color, it's easy to forget the sheer vastness of the sky. To the modern onlooker, a sunset may even seem visually unimpressive compared to the graphic renderings of movies or fancy light shows. But before such technology existed, each sunset must have been a mind-blowing revelation. It was the first and only time people ever witnessed such grand spectacles of shifting color on such a large scale.

Despite the technological advancements of the modern day, despite all the screens and lightbulbs and innovations, we are all still immensely dependent on the sun. Nothing can compare to sunlight when it comes to heating the world or providing energy to plants and crops. The sun's rising and setting

# MINDFULNESS

Before you start to watch the sunset, think about your time. How much space for quiet or enjoyment do you have in this current moment, in the rest of the day, in the span of your life? Think about what it means to "have time," and how these thoughts make you feel. Now, put those thoughts to the side and watch the sun as it begins to reach for the horizon. Let yourself notice things in the sky as they happen, and make a meal of the moment.

When the sunset is over, and the sky is dark, turn your mind once again to time. Not much time has passed since the start of the sun's setting, but perhaps your feelings are different. How do you feel about the time left in your day, or in your life? Does the subject of time, or what it means to make the most of time, feel different at all, and in what way? What does that mean for how you will live tomorrow?

is such a fundamental fact of life that we often take it for granted. But without its light or warmth, our planet would be unmoored from its natural cycles. No amount of technology could fix that.

## HARNESS WHAT WE HAVE

**B**efore humankind was even on this planet, the sun still set every evening, and long after we're gone, the sun will continue to put on its miraculous show. But it's important to realize that this display is not in service to us. Yes, the sun provides these great gifts, like warmth and light, but what we do with them is up to us. Humans of millennia past have interacted with the sun, harnessing its power to grow crops and use its progress across the sky to tell time. What would it look like for each of us, on an individual scale, to use sunlight as a way to maximize our well-being? For you, that might mean carving out time in your day to do nothing but soak up the sun, or rigging up solar panels to harness the sun's energy. The sky—and the sun—is the limit.

## HUMANS ARE A BLIP ON THIS EARTH

Compared to the cosmic longevity of the sun, humans have been around for virtually no time at all. Our species evolved sometime between 300,000 and 400,000 years ago. By the time *Homo sapiens* evolved, the sun had already been around for about 4.6 billion years.

There are many parallels between human existence and the cycle of the sun. Individual human lives are brief in the scheme of our species, in the same way that a single day is brief in the scheme of the sun's long existence. From the sun's perspective, humans have been around for a short while, but even that time is broken down into tinier segments, a string of life spans that pass in a flash. From our perspective, each day is short and each sunset is fleeting, but our appreciation for the phenomenon lasts and lasts.

## TUNE IN TO YOUR NATURAL RHYTHMS

*omo sapiens*, like most animals on
Earth, have tied their lifestyles to
the patterns of the sun. Its rising
and setting dictates how we as diurnal animals
(i.e., animals that are active during the day)
navigate our days.

The sun's fall toward the horizon has
traditionally been interpreted as a signal to
slow down, to seek shelter and rest. But that
association came about long before humans
discovered electricity, or even fire. Our bodies
have always listened to the surrounding world,
but what we hear has changed as humans
mold the landscape with industrialization and
new technology.

It would benefit us all to take stock of the
sun and listen. What does the early setting
sun after a bright winter day tell your body,
and how does that make you feel? What about
an early sunrise on a summer morning? Lis-
tening to your circadian rhythms and taking
your cues from your body and the sun are

13.8 BILLION YEARS AGO:

THE BIG BANG BRINGS THE UNIVERSE INTO EXISTENCE

4.603 BILLION YEARS AGO:

OUR SOLAR SYSTEM & SUN ARE FORMED

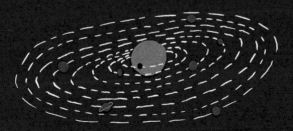

4.5 BILLION YEARS AGO:
EARTH IS FORMED

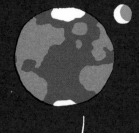

YOU, TODAY

300,000 YEARS AGO:
PRIMITIVE
HOMO SAPIENS
EVOLVED

160,000 YEARS AGO:
MODERN
HOMO SAPIENS
EVOLVED

practices that can put you back in touch with your body's preferred states of being. Living according to your natural clock is something like a dance, where you intuitively respond to the natural world's movements throughout the day. The rigid framework of societal clocks and calendars should not dictate your energy and productivity—that should be decided by your relationship with the world around you.

## APPRECIATE THE EVERYDAY

The lives of humans today look dramatically different from those just a hundred years ago, let alone from the beginning of our species. But in all that time, one constant in human experience has been the presence of the sun. Every generation has witnessed, if not admired, the beauty of a sunset. In some respect, an appreciation of the sun is almost a fundamental part of the human experience, and it will continue to be for as long as we live.

If you missed the opportunity to appreciate the sunset in all its glory in earlier chapters of your life, that's fine. But now that you know so much more about the sunset, make a point to appreciate it. By consistently noticing the natural wonders that exist all around us, you invite more magic, mindfulness, and serenity into every day.

DEC·1954

Maui '89

Ballantyne, Coco. "Fact or Fiction? Smog Creates Beautiful Sunsets." *Scientific American,* July 12, 2007. https://www.scientificamerican.com/article/fact-or-fiction-smog-creates-beautiful-sunsets/.

Brown, Evan Nicole. "Why Desert Sunsets Are Incredibly Colorful." *Atlas Obscura,* April 23, 2019. https://www.atlasobscura.com/articles/why-are-desert-sunsets-so-colorful.

Bushwick, Sophie. "Paintings of Sunsets Shed Light on Past Air Quality." *Scientific American,* March 25, 2014. https://www.scientificamerican.com/podcast/episode/paintings-of-sunsets-shed-light-on-past-air-quality/.

Corfidi, Stephen. "The Colors of Sunset and Twilight." NOAA/National Weather Service, Storm Prediction Center, September 2014. https://www.spc.noaa.gov/publications/corfidi/sunset/.

Helmenstine, Anne. "The Scientific Reason Why Hawaiian Sunsets Are So Beautiful." *Science Notes and Projects,* May 10, 2021. https://sciencenotes.org/the-scientific-reason-why-hawaiian-sunsets-are-so-beautiful/.

Krukarius. "Light Scattering in the Earth's Atmosphere Part 2 – Why Is the Sky Blue and How the Sky Colour Change?" *MkrGeo,* September 30, 2021. http://www.mkrgeo-blog.com/light-scattering-in-the-earths-atmosphere-part-2-why-is-the-sky-blue-and-how-the-sky-color-changes/.

McClure, Bruce. "Longest Sunsets around the Solstices." *EarthSky,* June 18, 2021. https://earthsky.org/tonight/longest-sunsets-around-solstices/.